FIRE's GUIDE TO
RELIGIOUS LIBERTY ON CAMPUS

FIRE's GUIDES TO
STUDENT RIGHTS ON CAMPUS

www.thefireguides.org

FIRE's Guide to Religious Liberty on Campus

FIRE's Guide to Student Fees, Funding, and Legal Equality
on Campus

FIRE's Guide to Due Process and Fair Procedure on Campus

FIRE's Guide to Free Speech on Campus

FIRE's Guide to First-Year Orientation and
to Thought Reform on Campus

FIRE

David French
President

FIRE's GUIDE TO

RELIGIOUS LIBERTY ON CAMPUS

David A. French

FOUNDATION FOR INDIVIDUAL RIGHTS IN EDUCATION
Philadelphia

FIRE's Know Your Rights Program and FIRE's *Guides* to Student Rights on Campus are made possible by grants from the John Templeton Foundation, The Achelis Foundation, The Joseph Harrison Jackson Foundation, and Earhart Foundation. The Foundation for Individual Rights in Education gratefully acknowledges their support.

ISBN 0-9724712-0-0
Library of Congress Cataloging-in-Publication data is available upon request.

Published in the United States by:

      Foundation for Individual Rights in Education
      601 Walnut Street, Suite 510
      Philadelphia, PA 19106

Cover art printed by permission of the Norman Rockwell Family Agency

Copyright © 1943 the Norman Rockwell Family Entities

Cover and interior design by Eliz. Anne O'Donnell

Manufactured in USA

CONTENTS

PREFACE

Students should know their rights and liberties, and they need to be better informed and better equipped about how to assert and defend these precious things. The protectors of students' rights and liberties—those faculty, administrators, parents, alumni, friends, citizens, advisers, and attorneys who care about such vital matters—should understand the threats to freedom and legal equality on our campuses, the moral and legal means of combating those threats, and the acquired experience of recent years. To that end, the Foundation for Individual Rights in Education (FIRE) offers this *Guide to Religious Liberty on Campus*, part of a series of such guides designed to restore individual rights and the values of a free society to our nation's colleges and universities. These guides also should remind those who write, revise, and enforce campus policies of the legal and moral constraints that restrict their authority. The sooner that colleges and universities understand their legal and moral obligations to a free and decent society, the less need there will be for guides such as these.

INTRODUCTION

Consider Tufts University, Grinnell College, Williams College, Ball State University, Whitman College, Middlebury College, Randolph-Macon Women's College, the State University of New York at Oswego, Wichita State University, Castleton State College, and Purdue University. This roll call of colleges and universities is merely a partial list of schools that have sought to either ban outright or heavily regulate the activities of religious students or religious student groups. These institutions have charged students and student groups with, among other things, violating school policies on the inclusion of gays and lesbians, violating school regulations of speech, and, ironically, "discriminating" on the basis of religion. In the modern university, it is now considered improper for religious groups to use religious principles to make religious decisions about their religious missions.

Many students accustomed to being in an active religious majority in their high schools and communities will find an almost complete reversal of their circumstances when they enter the world of American higher education. Just as religious majorities should respect—morally and legally—the rights of unbelievers or dissenters back in their home communities, so should colleges and universities respect the rights of religious students on America's campuses. The tragedy of power is that we usually see the abuses of others, but we too rarely see our own.

In many ways, religious liberty is now center stage in the battle for freedom on campus. For too many administrators, religious students are particularly convenient targets. After all, they think and behave in ways that many other students don't understand; they tend to be very small minorities on most campuses; and—by religious conviction—they often resist even the most heavy-handed repression. For all the talk about diversity and tolerance, too few students and faculty care when people of faith are given fewer rights than other groups, and such believers enjoy scant support when they engage in religious practices deemed "regressive" by their more "progressive" peers. In the eyes of the modern academic community, the fewer "fanatics"—of the "wrong" kind—the better.

All friends of liberty must stand against this kind of oppression, and doubly so when it is selective. Selective repression is particularly dangerous, of course, because when repression is applied across the board and equally to all groups, everyone recognizes and begins to work against it. When repression is selective, too many just stand by. The free marketplace of ideas—where individuals and groups may peacefully and without coercion follow their own consciences—nurtures a true civil society capable of peaceful change.

Universities, as we shall see in the pages that follow, have a moral—and often legal—obligation to their students' freedom of conscience and freedom of thought. Religious liberty—including the freedom to disbelieve— is a fundamental freedom. Universities are places where ideas should be exchanged, discussed, analyzed, and debated. They should not be centers of a one true, politically acceptable agenda, let alone of such an agenda enforced by secret tribunals. Universities that promise academic freedom and pluralism may not in good conscience banish this or that orthodoxy or heterodoxy from their public arenas.

This guide is a major step in the battle for religious freedom and the rights of conscience on campus. Its purpose is to educate students, faculty, administrators, and the public on the origins and nature of religious liberty in our society and, more particularly, on our campuses. The first section of this guide defines the scope of religious liberty generally. The second section explains religious liberty and the rights of conscience in the public and private university. The final section outlines the most common threats to basic religious liberty and provides basic guidance for those who seek to respond to such threats.

RELIGIOUS LIBERTY: A BASIC PRIMER

The Right To Religious Liberty

America is a nation that, from its founding, has proclaimed the rights of religious liberty and religious diversity. In the eighteenth century, after hundreds of years of religious wars, persecutions, and hatreds in the west, the deepest minds of our civilization, religious and secular, asserted the need for religious liberty and its consequence, religious pluralism. For James Madison and so many of the American Founders, religious liberty was an inalienable right.

Before it even addresses freedom of speech and of the press, the First Amendment of the United States Constitution recognizes freedom of religion. It declares, "Congress shall make no law . . . respecting an establishment of religion or prohibiting the free exercise thereof." This simple phrase fulfills two vital purposes, as the

U.S. Supreme Court explained in its celebrated decision in *Cantwell v. Connecticut* (1940). First, the "Establishment Clause" of the First Amendment "forestalls compulsion by law of the acceptance of any creed or the practice of any form of worship." In other words, freedom of conscience and the freedom to choose and to belong to a religion or religious organization, or to none at all, cannot be restricted by law. The government may not establish a religious orthodoxy, nor advance a specific religion, nor promote religion in general. This principle—that the government must be neutral on the subject of religion—has been confirmed many times by the Supreme Court, most recently in the case of *Zelman v. Simmons-Harris* (2002). In its decision, the Court affirmed the constitutionality of school voucher programs in which the state gives funds for tuition assistance to individual citizens who then may choose to spend it at either secular or religious schools. The Court held that such programs are constitutional because they have neither the "purpose" nor the "effect" of "advancing or inhibiting religion." The program, said the Court, "is neutral in all respects toward religion." Second, the "Free Exercise Clause" protects the freedom of religious citizens to practice a

> The *Establishment Clause* of the First Amendment prevents the state from forcing any form of religion or religious creed on the individual.

chosen form of religion. The religion clauses of the First Amendment assure liberty not only to the citizen's religious sensibilities and practice, but also to the citizen's moral, ethical and conscientious precepts when these function for the nonbeliever in the same ways that religion functions for the believer. "Thus," the Supreme Court made clear in *Cantwell*, "the Amendment embraces two concepts— freedom to believe and freedom to act." In short, the meaning of the religion clauses was stated clearly by the Supreme Court in *Zelman*: The state may not "advance" (Establishment Clause) nor "inhibit" (Free Exercise Clause) religion.

> The *Free Exercise Clause* of the First Amendment protects individuals and groups from government interference in the practice of their religion.

The "freedom to act," the freedom protected by the Free Exercise Clause of the First Amendment, is not unlimited, however. The government—and that includes *public* universities, because they are governmental entities whose powers are kept in check by the Bill of Rights—may restrict religious liberty under certain circumstances.

The precise extent of the government's ability to regulate religious practice is the subject of much misunderstanding. Recent changes in the law, particularly in the civil rights area, have led many university administrators (and their legal advisers) to believe that they have vast authority—even an obligation—to regulate the religious practices of students, faculty members, and religious organizations. This view, however, is profoundly mistaken. In fact, the recent legal trend has been precisely the opposite: toward an *expansion* of the religious liberty of individuals and organizations, of believers and unbelievers alike.

There is a widespread notion that religious belief and practice must be curtailed to protect the civil rights of others. Laws and regulations indeed extend what are commonly called "rights" to individuals. The Bill of Rights (the first ten amendments to the U.S. Constitution), however, is the foundation and heart of our liberties. The First Amendment explicitly states a set of civil liberties protected by the Constitution, in particular, the freedoms of speech, press, and religion. These liberties set the boundaries to claims of newer and newer "rights." Individuals claim "rights" of equal access to group membership and leadership or "rights" of never being "offended" or "excluded." In short, some individuals believe that "civil rights" might somehow trump the "civil liberties" of those who exercise such constitutionally protected liberties as freedom of speech, freedom of the press, freedom of religion, and what follows from them, freedom of association.

For example, the Boy Scouts of America were recently involved in litigation over a state's attempt to compel them to admit gay scouts and scout leaders. The U.S. Supreme Court, however, ruled that the Scouts have a right to determine the nature of their own voluntary association, social message, and organizational mission. The issue, of course, is not whether governmental authorities, a majority of citizens, FIRE, or strong minorities agree or disagree with the Scouts, but whether private groups like the Scouts, including gay political or social groups, may determine their own mission and membership.

Most recent confusion about religious liberty has arisen from the issue of an appropriate legal "test" for government action. Obviously, the government may restrict religious practices that include murder, theft, and other felonies, but where do we draw the line? What uniform standard will be used to judge the legality of government limitations on religious practice? This standard has changed twice in the last forty years.

In 1963, the Supreme Court decided the case of *Sherbert v. Verner*. In *Sherbert*, as it is known, a woman challenged a state's decision to deny her request for unemployment benefits. The state's decision was based on her refusal to work on Saturday, the Sabbath Day of her faith. The Supreme Court held that the state violated the Free Exercise Clause of the First Amendment when it required, in exchange for a government benefit (unemployment compensation), a change in religious practice (nonobservance of Sabbath rest).

This decision, by itself, was unremarkable. What set *Sherbert* apart, however, was the legal standard that it introduced. Justice William Brennan, writing for the Court, stated that if a government action imposes a significant burden on religious practice, that action could be justified only if

1) it advances a "compelling state interest"; and
2) "no alternative forms of regulation" would suffice. *Unless both requirements of that test could be satisfied, the government's action would be unconstitutional and invalid.*

This standard is known, among lawyers and in courts, as "strict scrutiny." It is not sufficient for the state to wish to regulate religion to achieve this or that "good." Rather, to overcome the powerful presumption in favor of religious liberty, the state must have the most urgent—that is, "compelling"—need to act, and it must show that this need could not be satisfied by some other more narrowly tailored and less intrusive regulation. Further, the regulation may not be simply a disguised attempt to interfere with a religious practice.

The standard set by *Sherbert*—although the Supreme Court occasionally, but rarely, departs from it—marked a very significant advance in "free exercise" jurisprudence and provided vital protection for religious liberty. It was very difficult for the government to prove that "compelling" governmental interests justified specific regulations restricting religious liberty. Courts became and remain justifiably reluctant to believe that a government is "compelled" to limit core individual freedoms.

In 1990, however, the standard underwent a change whose scope and application is both controversial and widely misunderstood. In *Employment Division v. Smith*, the Supreme Court decided the case of two individuals punished for the religious use of peyote, an illegal drug. Peyote is ingested for sacramental purposes during some ceremonies of the Native American Church. The Supreme Court upheld the State of Oregon's decision to deny unemployment benefits to the individuals, and, in so doing, it changed more than two decades of precedent.

Again, the crucial issue is the standard that the Court established in *Smith*, as this case is known. That new standard was that the government was not required to satisfy "strict scrutiny"—that is, to demonstrate both that its regulations furthered a "compelling state interest" and that no alternative forms of regulation would serve the same purpose. Instead, the government needed only to demonstrate that its restriction of religious practice arose *not from any attack on religion, but on the basis of a valid law, generally applicable to all citizens*—in legalese, a "valid and neutral law of general applicability." In other words, the Free Exercise Clause, by itself, would not protect individuals from state restrictions on religious practice (such as the use of an illegal drug) if the state was not specifically targeting religion, but was simply enforcing a law equally applicable to all. (By such reasoning, some argued, the state could have banned sacramental wine in Catholic and other masses during Prohibition.)

In the controversy that followed this decision, many governmental bodies, in a rush to regulate religious practice, chose to ignore the clear force with which many aspects of the Supreme Court's ruling preserved certain strict standards. First and foremost, the Court had stated emphatically that state action toward religious organizations must be *neutral*. In other words, the government—although freed from the "compelling state interest" standard—did not have the right to enact laws designed primarily (or even partially) to suppress the practice of religion. For example, in *Church of the Lukumi Babalu Aye, Inc. v. Hialeah* (1993), the Supreme Court overturned the City of Hialeah's attempt to ban ritual animal sacrifice, finding that the purpose of the statute was the suppression of Santeria religious worship (practiced by some Caribbean-Americans).

Religious individuals and groups can *enhance* the level of constitutional protection by combining their First Amendment *free exercise* rights with other constitutional rights—such as *freedom of speech* and *freedom of association*.

While *Smith* weakened the force of free exercise claims, religious individuals and groups could strengthen those claims by "coupling" or "bundling" them with other constitutional rights. If religious individuals were confronted by a government policy that restricted their religious practice, they often argued rightly that the policy violated *not only* free exercise rights, but also rights to free speech and free association. If, indeed, state actions affect other constitutional rights while regulating religious practice, then the standard changes, and "strict scrutiny" again will often apply to official actions, thus reestablishing the highest hurdle for government activity to overcome. ("Freedom of association" is not explicitly mentioned in the Constitution. However, the Supreme Court long has held that the right to free speech is virtually meaningless without a corresponding right to form organizations, such as the NAACP, the Christian Coalition, the ACLU, and the Republican and Democratic Parties, for example, in order to advance particular viewpoints and to associate with others of like mind. In short, "freedom of association"—without which freedom of speech would be profoundly weakened—is implied by the Constitu-

The First Amendment's *Free Speech Clause* limits the ability of the government to interfere with your right to speak your mind. Courts have ruled that religious speech and worship are forms of expression protected by the *Free Speech Clause*.

Freedom of association protects your right to form organizations, to advance particular viewpoints, and to associate with others of like mind. Courts have ruled that free association rights apply to religious individuals and groups.

tion's Bill of Rights. Indeed, there exists an explicit Constitutional right to free assembly. The First Amendment protects "the right of the people peacefully to assemble," a self-evident protection for private organizations.)

Those standards—government neutrality and strict scrutiny when other constitutional rights are involved—critically limit the state's regulation of religious practice. Administrators, faculties, and student judiciaries at public colleges and universities—eager to impose their secular orthodoxies on campus—often view the *Smith* decision as granting them a free hand to regulate religious practice on campus. Nothing could be further from the truth. *Campus policies that inhibit religious practices almost always inhibit the rights of free speech, association, and assembly.*

Furthermore, and this has affected more recent Court rulings, the *Smith* decision produced a very intense and critical response from the public, from Congress, and from both mainstream and minority religious groups. Indeed, Congress passed and President Bill Clinton signed legislation to correct what they saw as the serious ills of *Smith*, but the Supreme Court judged such

attempts to be unconstitutional on grounds of the separation of powers. (The Court found that Congress did
not have the power to expand or to contract constitutional rights.) Nonetheless, the Court began to understand that it had entered dangerous territory in limiting
the religious rights not only of Native American Church
members, but also of *all* Americans. In subsequent cases
the Court has pulled back dramatically, narrowing the
application of the *Smith* doctrine and keeping much of
"strict scrutiny" intact. For example, in the *Hialeah* case
mentioned above, Justice Kennedy's opinion reads as a
virtual "how-to" guide for lawyers who wish to circum-
vent *Smith* and apply strict scrutiny to government
decisions. *Hialeah* restores strict scrutiny to many situ-
ations: when a law specifi-cally mentions religious
practice, when there are hints of antireligious mo-tives
by the government, or when the law affects reli-gious
practice alone.

> Even in light of recent limits on the *Free Exercise Clause*, courts will still give *strict scrutiny* to government regulations that *mention religious practice*, that are *motivated by antireligious bias* or *have an impact upon religious practice alone*.

In the wake of the *Hialeah* case, it is now
unclear whether the *Smith* test retains much viability. If
the government takes an action or enacts a law that
impinges upon religious rights alone, then there is a

good chance that *Hialeah* would offer the religious individual or group the protection of strict scrutiny. If the government action implicates more than just religious rights (such as rights to free speech or free association), then religious individuals or groups will be able to "bundle" their religious rights with these other rights and again be protected by strict scrutiny.

For many first-rate legal minds, then, the test established by *Sherbert*, that of "compelling state interest," is still unsettled in its scope, and may still apply to a broad range of cases. What is wholly clear, however, is that for the state legally to regulate religious practice, the restriction in question must, at the very least, be neutral *and* must not inhibit the exercise of other, related constitutional freedoms. *If a public university discriminates among viewpoints by limiting specific religious practices or by denying to one religious group or individual a benefit that it offers to other religious groups or to secular organizations, then its actions will almost certainly be deemed unlawful.*

What Does It Mean, Legally, To Be "Religious"?

The right to religious liberty is not limited to members of mainstream churches, or to fundamentalist Protestants, or to observant Catholics, or to Orthodox Jews. Indeed, the rights of religious liberty are not the exclusive realm of those who would define themselves as particularly "religious." It is a common misperception that only those individuals who attend church, mosque, or synagogue regularly either care about or are affected by issues of religious liberty.

The right to the free exercise of "religion" is not limited by conventional or orthodox understandings of the nature of "religion" or "religious practice." Indeed, the Free Exercise Clause protects both the beliefs and practices of those whose religion may not be based upon belief in God (nontheists) and those whose religion is founded upon belief in a Supreme Being (theists). The Supreme Court has made clear that freedom of religion includes a wide variety of deeply held nontheistic beliefs that play a role in someone's life similar to that played by the belief in God in the life of a more traditionally religious person. The religion clauses of the First Amendment are best understood as guardians of *everyone's* freedom of conscience—and of *every - one's* particular ideas of ultimate meaning and ultimate spiritual authority, including the freedom of those who disbelieve.

> The *Free Exercise Clause* protects both the beliefs and practices of those whose religion may not be based upon a belief in God (*nontheists*) and those whose religion is founded upon a belief in a Supreme Being (*theists*).

Although the Supreme Court has never precisely defined "religion," it has given religious liberty stun-

> The *Free Exercise Clause* protects even those individuals who do not define themselves specifically as "religious."

ningly broad scope. First, as noted, one does not have to define oneself specifically as "religious" to receive constitutional religious protections. In *United States v. Seeger* (1965), the Court held that a "sincere and meaningful belief which occupies in the life of its possessor a place parallel to that filled by God" could be classified as religious.

In the groundbreaking case of *Welsh v. United States* (1970), the Supreme Court built on its decision in *Seeger*. It reviewed the appeal of an individual who had sought conscientious objector status under a statute that exempted from military service individuals who, by reason of "religious training and belief," were conscientiously opposed to war in any form. Mr. Welsh, however, had stated that he could not affirm or deny belief in a "Supreme Being," and he had struck the words "my religious training" from the form that requested the exemption. He was convicted for refusing to accept induction into the armed services. Reversing that conviction, the Supreme Court found that Welsh's beliefs—including his belief that taking any life was morally wrong—were more than "a merely personal honor code" and were held with "the strength of more traditional religious convictions." Consequently, he was entitled to receive the "religious" exemption to military service.

Second, if individuals do define themselves as religious, they do not have to belong to a theistic religion to receive the protection of the religion clauses of the Constitution. The Supreme Court specifically rejected any limitation of "religion" to theistic religions in *Torcaso v. Watkins* (1961), a case invalidating a Maryland constitutional provision that required appointees to public office to declare a belief in the existence of God. In extending protection to a Secular Humanist challenging the Maryland law, Justice Hugo Black, writing for the Court, specifically listed a number of prominent, nontheistic religions, citing "Buddhism, Taoism, Ethical Culture, Secular Humanism, and others."

> You do not have to belong to a theistic religion to receive the protection of the religion clauses of the First Amendment; nor do you have to belong to an "organized" religious group.

Third, religious protections are not limited to members of an "organized" religious group. In *Frazee v. Illinois Department of Employment Security* (1989), the Supreme Court allowed a Christian who was not a member of an established religion or sect to receive unemployment benefits despite his refusal to work on Sundays. Justice White, writing for a unanimous Court, explained that the protection of the Free Exercise Clause was *not* limited to those "responding to the commands of a particular religious organization."

Fourth, individuals can assert religious liberty claims even if their views differ from those of their church or from other members of their religion. In *Thomas v. Review Board of Indiana Employment Security Division* (1981), the Supreme Court reversed Indiana's decision to deny unemployment benefits to a Jehovah's Witness who quit his job because his religious beliefs forbade participation in the production of armaments. Indiana courts had upheld the decision to deny benefits, finding that Thomas's views regarding the production of tank turrets differed from those of other Jehovah's Witnesses and were not those of "his religion." The Supreme Court emphatically disagreed with such a requirement of conformity, holding that "it is not within the judicial function and judicial competence to inquire whether the petitioner or his fellow worker more correctly perceived the commands of their common faith. Courts are not arbiters of scriptural interpretation."

> You can assert religious liberty claims even if your views differ from those of your church or from other members of your religion.

These decisions may be seen as the Supreme Court's recognition that not only are minority religions entitled to constitutional protection (a doctrine that has long been established), but that quite unconventional religions, and even what might be called "substitutes" for religion, are entitled to the same protection. The doctrine of protected religious diversity has taken profound hold in constitutional jurisprudence.

Religious liberty, thus, exists for all individuals—believers and unbelievers—who hold sincere and meaningful beliefs about ultimate issues in life. Such beliefs are of transcendent importance to many individuals. State actions that strike at those beliefs, that offend one's conscience, may very well involve and implicate the First Amendment. Citizens should not limit their liberty—nor shrink back in the face of repression—simply because their consciences place them outside the mainstream of American life, or because their "church" is small, or because no one else shares their views. Liberties exist for a minority as much they do for the majority. That is the nature of a free and decent society.

Public Versus Private: The Limits of Constitutional Protection

To this point, this discussion of religious liberty has focused on protections offered by the First Amendment and constitutional law, which restrict the behavior of the state, including public colleges and universities. However, it is as important to understand what the Constitution does not protect as it is to understand what it does protect. The Constitution of the United States protects individual freedoms from *government* interference. It does not, as a rule, protect individual freedoms

The Constitution of the United States protects individual freedoms from *government* interference. It does not, as a rule, protect individual freedoms from interference by *private* organizations.

from interference by *private* organizations, such as corporations or private universities. For example, while a state could never create a Christian academy or mandate attendance at Bible classes and chapel services, voluntary private organizations have a right to do precisely such things. Thousands of church-based schools and colleges exist in America, and these private, religious organizations are free to mandate religious practice, to forbid what they judge to be immoral behavior, and to restrict speech. Private organizations have freedoms denied to government—the freedom to impinge on constitutional liberties that are protected from governmental interference. Indeed, the Constitution guarantees the "free exercise" of those liberties, because we could not have a free and pluralistic society if private organizations did not enjoy this freedom of belief and practice.

The case of private universities serves well to illustrate this distinction. Despite their theoretical freedom to restrict speech, private, secular universities once prided themselves on being special havens for free expression—religious, political, and cultural. Indeed, many of America's great private educational institutions have traditionally chosen to allow greater freedom than public universities, even permitting forms of expression that public universities could legally prohibit. Until recently, few places allowed more discussion, more diverse student groups, and more cutting-edge expression than America's elite private universities.

Unfortunately, that now has changed. Even America's best private, secular, and liberal arts colleges and universities are becoming centers of censorship and repression on behalf of campus orthodoxies. Speech codes, sweeping "anti-harassment" regulations, and broad and vague anti-discrimination policies increasingly have stifled discourse. More and more, vaunted Ivy League and similar universities are becoming places where a vast number of religious traditions and ideas are simply not welcome. Many secular, private schools appear as committed to their anti-religious orthodoxy as Bob Jones University is to its fundamentalist Christianity and anti-secularism.

> Freed from Constitutional restraint, some of America's best private, secular, and liberal arts colleges and universities are becoming centers of censorship and repression on behalf of campus orthodoxies.

Although these private institutions are not bound by the First Amendment, there still are limits to what harm they may do to those who seek to exercise their religious liberty. Contrary to the wishes of many administrators

Private universities do not have unlimited power over their students. They still must comply with a complex web of federal and state laws that provides considerable protections for the religious rights of individuals and groups.

and faculty members, private organizations do not possess unlimited power over the lives of members of those communities. Beyond the Constitution, we still live in a society of both common and statutory law. Here, a complex web of federal and state statutes and state common law provides considerable protections for the religious rights of individuals and groups.

For example, Title VII of the Civil Rights Act of 1964 is a federal statute that prohibits private employers from discriminating against any employee "because of such individual's race, color, religion, sex, or national origin." ("Titles" are parts or sections of an Act.) While someone may be fired from a job for loudly criticizing a supervisor, a person may not be fired or otherwise discriminated against simply for being a man, or a black, or a Methodist. This provision is the legal source of workplace sexual harassment laws and regulations.

Statutes are laws written by legislatures—both state and federal—that often limit a university's ability to act against the interests of its students.

Another sort of protection arises from conditions that Congress may place on private organizations that choose to accept and use federal funding for various programs. Title IX, for example, famous for its impact on collegiate athletic programs, prohibits sexual discrimination at any school (private or public) that receives federal funds: "No person in the United States shall, on the basis of sex, be excluded from participation in, be denied the benefits of, or be subjected to discrimination under any education program or activity receiving Federal financial assistance." (Here, however, Congress recognized the necessity of not interfering with the free exercise of religion by exempting from the act "educational institutions of religious organizations with contrary religious tenets.") Title VI prohibits discrimination on the basis of race and ethnicity: "No person in the United States shall, on the ground of race, color, or national origin, be excluded from participation in, be denied the benefits of, or be subjected to discrimination under any program or activity receiving Federal financial assistance." Since virtually every university in America receives some amount of federal funds, they are almost all bound by these restrictions. Further, individual states have passed their own laws, some of which simply mirror federal laws and constitutional requirements, and some of which create their own unique requirements.

For students at private colleges and universities, however, the most relevant law is state common law. The phrase "common law" is an ancient term for legal rules that are created, adapted, and applied not by legislatures or city councils but by juries and judges over a long period of time. Most arose from the rules that worked in keeping the peace and fairness of civil society. The common law typically encompasses legal rules that govern contracts and torts (that is, things that cause harm), or, more technically, "civil wrongs" (such as product liability, libel, medical malpractice, or car accidents involving negligence or recklessness). Often, the origins of a specific element of common law—such as the imposition of monetary liability for negligent acts that harm others—stretch back hundreds of years to the fifteenth and sixteenth centuries. Without common law, there would have been no rules but the right of the strongest. Individual states have each incorporated varying degrees of common law into their legal systems. In general, however, common law prevents a private college or university from committing fraud or breach of contract in its dealings with individuals, or from harming them wrongfully.

State *common law* rules can provide considerable protection to private school students. In general, the common law prevents a private college or university from committing *fraud* or *breach of contract* in its dealings with individuals and groups.

Given this complex system, which varies state by state,

it is difficult to talk about "student rights" as if they were the same for everyone, everywhere. Students at Brown University in Rhode Island have common law rights substantially different from students at Harvard University in Massachusetts or at Vanderbilt University in Tennessee. Different states have different legal doctrines.

To understand your rights as a student, therefore, you must ask the following questions: 1) Is my college or university a public institution? If so, its actions are limited by the First Amendment and by federal and state statutes and state common law. If it is a private institution, it still will be limited by federal and state statutes and state common law. Thus, you will need to know 2) what are my statutory rights? and 3) what are my state common law rights? To help answer the third question, concerning your common law rights, it will be useful to know what the school itself says in its student handbooks, catalogues, and disciplinary codes. In these, you will find its promises to its students, many of which may be legally binding. In the pages that follow, this guide will explain in more detail the significance of these questions and will provide some universal, generalized guidance that will help you to identify some of the primary threats to religious liberty on the modern campus and to plan responses to potential persecution, oppression, or unequal treatment.

RELIGIOUS LIBERTY IN THE UNIVERSITY

This section is subdivided into two distinct parts: 1) a discussion of religious liberty in the public university, where the Constitution applies and provides comprehensive protections; and 2) a discussion of religious liberty in the private university, where state statutes and the rules of common law govern.

Religious Liberty in the Public University

For the public university student concerned with religious liberty, the Free Exercise Clause of the Constitution is much more critical than the Establishment Clause. (It is very unlikely that a public university will attempt to establish Lutheranism as an official religion, for example. It is more likely that it will seek to restrict the free practice of a religion.) As explained earlier, the Free Exercise Clause protects religious individuals and groups from specifically targeted, anti-religious state action. In other words, a public university may not institute any policy designed primarily (or even partially) to suppress the practice of religion.

That means, among many other things, that no public university may restrict freedom of religion indirectly, by adopting some official campus secular political orthodoxy—"multiculturalism" or "diversity," for example—which it then uses to restrict religious beliefs and practices that supposedly betray the "official" campus ideology. Directly restricting religion and insisting that all students adhere to some official campus orthodoxy are two sides of the same coin and are unlawful for the same reason: they violate the First Amendment.

Recall that the Constitution permits religious groups to "couple" their free exercise rights with other constitutional rights. This means that if religious individuals or groups are confronted with a university policy that discriminates against their religious message, then they may not only claim a violation of their free exercise rights but also of their rights to free speech and to free association. In such a circumstance, it becomes much more difficult for the university's policies to prevail.

Because of the mutually strengthening and sustaining relationship of free speech, free association, and the free exercise of religion, public universities are severely limited in their ability to regulate campus religious practice.

Public universities are severely limited in their ability to regulate campus religious practice. The key word that governs a public university's obligations is *neutrality*. If its behavior offers a benefit to individuals or organizations with a particular viewpoint or religion, then it must offer that same benefit or access to other individuals or organizations with different viewpoints or religions.

The key word that governs a public university's obligations is *neutrality*. If its behavior offers a benefit to individuals or organizations with a particular viewpoint or religion, then it must offer that same benefit or access to other individuals or organizations with different viewpoints or religions. Because they are agents of the government, public colleges and universities may not engage in *viewpoint discrimination*.

You should know that there is a long-standing controversy between two different views of the proper application of the Establishment Clause. As discussed earlier, the Supreme Court has made it clear—as recently as in its "school vouchers" case (*Zelman v. Simmons-Harris*) in 2002—that the government must remain "neutral in all respects toward religion" and may not enact laws "that have the 'purpose' or 'effect' of advancing or inhibiting religion." The controversy is over the meaning and scope of state "neutrality," and, in particular, over cases in which government seems to "advance" religion by such things as putting up Christmas trees in public places or paying chaplains, with public funds, to open legislative sessions and other public events. Some individuals see such acts as violating the Establishment Clause. Other individuals view such cases as either trivial or, at their core, secular and not at all in conflict with the Establishment Clause.

This Guide does not seek to resolve the controversy as to precisely where the line should be drawn to define state neutrality. Rather, it seeks to give students practical advice about how they can protect their own right to believe and practice their own chosen religions—or none at all—without official interference or penalty—except in the face of compelling social and governmental interests that justify restrictions on practice, though never on belief. For the state, given the doctrine of "neutrality," neither religion nor irreligion enjoys any advantage over the other; they are of equal status in their rights and freedoms. Religious students often look, above all, to the Free Exercise Clause ("don't stop me from practicing my religion"). Nonreligious students often look, above all, to the Establishment Clause ("don't try to influence me to believe in or practice a religion or any belief system"). Both believers and nonbelievers often agree, however, that separation of church and state is vital to civic and to religious life, many believers concluding that such separation protects religion from the secularism inherent in government. The Supreme Court, at any rate, insists on the concept of state neutrality in matters of religion. For nonbelievers, this arms them to argue that public universities may neither favor nor promote religion over irreligion or secularism. For religious students, this arms them to argue that public universities may not interfere with their religious belief and practice, even if such practice has the incidental effect of offending or excluding others.

Several major Supreme Court cases illustrate the principle of viewpoint neutrality. The first, *Widmar v. Vincent* (1981), held that once a university opens its facilities to a broad spectrum of student groups, it may not then deny religious organizations that same access. This principle was reaffirmed in *Lamb's Chapel v. Center Moriches Union Free School* (1993), a case involving a public high school that denied religious organizations equal access to school facilities. The Supreme Court's conclusion was unanimous: "[I]t discriminates on the basis of viewpoint to permit school property to be used for the presentation of all views about family issues and child-rearing except those dealing with the subject matter from a religious standpoint."

> If a public university opens its facilities to use by political or cultural student groups, then it must allow religious individuals and groups *equal access* to those facilities.

Under the authority of *Widmar* and *Lamb's Chapel*, public universities that open gymnasiums, classrooms, auditoriums, and dorm facilities for use by groups as diverse as College Democrats, African-American Student Unions, anti-International Monetary Fund protest groups, feminists, and literary societies may not close those same facilities to religious organizations. Any university that attempts such discrimination is in clear violation of the law. Indeed, these other groups may rightly use the principles laid out in this guide in order to attain equal rights on those rare campuses that favor religious groups and discriminate against secular political groups. The nature and virtue of this is precisely that it protects everyone equally.

In fact, the principle of equal access is one of the most firmly established doctrines in constitutional law. As recently as the summer of 2001, the Supreme Court ruled that public schools must offer equal access to religious groups not only in colleges and high schools, but also in *elementary schools*. This case, called *Good News Club v. Milford Central School*, firmly and definitively removes any doubt about religious students' access to public facilities. *Every* religious student or group at *every* level of schooling is entitled to the same access to school facilities as secular students or groups. If a school opens its facilities to political or cultural clubs, it cannot shut those doors to religious students.

The principle of neutrality extends not only to the use

of facilities, but also to the use of university funds. In *Rosenberger v. University of Virginia* (1995), the University of Virginia authorized payments from a Student Activities Fund for the printing costs of publications by certain student groups. This payment program was utilized by a wide variety of student groups to print a great diversity of publications espousing political, social, and even religious views. Although the university supported a wide range of groups, including Jewish and Shinto publications, it refused to support the publication of a Christian magazine.

In response, the Supreme Court found that the university was guilty of unconstitutional viewpoint discrimination: "Having offered to pay the third-party contractors on behalf of private speakers who convey their own messages, the University may not silence the expression of selected viewpoints."

In fact, *viewpoint neutrality* is an absolute precondition to any public funding for student organizations. In the case of *University of Wisconsin v. Southworth* (2000), the Supreme Court provided a perfect description of the neutrality requirement. In *Southworth*, a University of Wisconsin student challenged the University's mandatory student activity fee, alleging that to force him to fund student groups whose political and ideological speech he found offensive violated his First Amendment rights. Although the Supreme Court agreed that a mandatory fee involved the student's First Amendment rights, it held that those rights were not being violated *as long as the university allocated the funds on a neutral basis.* In Justice

Sandra Day O'Connor's words: "Viewpoint neutrality is the justification for requiring the student to pay the fee in the first instance and for ensuring the integrity of the program's operation once the funds have been collected."

> Just as public universities must offer religious groups equal access to campus *facilities*, they must also offer equal access to university *funds*. All university funds must be allocated on a *viewpoint neutral* basis.

In sum, public universities that offer benefits to nonreligious "expressive organizations" on campus (an "expressive organization" is one that exists, at least in part, for the purpose of expressing a particular viewpoint) may not deny the same benefit to other students or groups simply because their viewpoint happens to be religious. This is a valuable application of the general principle—one might dub it the "Golden Rule" of constitutional decision-making—that citizens are entitled to equality before the law. That principle is one of the essential foundations of our liberty. It is what the drafters of the Fourteenth Amendment meant when they wrote that no state may "deny to any person within its jurisdiction the equal protection of the laws."

Campus religious organizations do face one form of legal jeopardy that, some have argued, makes the "neutrality principle" inapplicable. Most contemporary legal attacks on religion make use of laws or regulations that were not, in fact, specifically designed to work against religion. These legal weapons instead are, for the most part, "neutral laws of general applicability" that simply are applied in ways that defeat religious practice. The perfect example, by its relevance to student religious groups, would be a university policy that prohibits discrimination on the basis of sexual orientation. A university would argue that its policy is simply a "neutral, general law" applicable to everyone: biology professors may not refuse to hire lesbian teaching assistants; the football team may not exclude gay linebackers; and campus religious organizations may not bar gay members. In other words, the rule was not designed to target a particular religion, or religion in general, but was instead created to protect all individuals from any discrimination based on sexual orientation.

> Because college anti-discrimination policies apply to all members of the campus community, they may be considered neutral and generally applicable. Religious students and groups must rely on free association rights to preserve their religious liberties.

The difference between this kind of situation and the situation faced by the religious individuals in *Widmar* and *Rosenberger* is obvious. The plaintiffs in those cases were attacking policies that were designed to benefit everyone *except* religious organizations. The viewpoint discrimination was clear. Most campus anti-discrimination policies are designed to apply to everyone, *including* religious organizations. In such a case, there appears to be no viewpoint discrimination whatsoever.

Prior to the Supreme Court's recent decisions in *Hurley v. Irish-American Gay, Lesbian and Bisexual Group of Boston* (1995) and in *Boy Scouts of America v. Dale* (2000), it was unclear whether an expressive or religious organization's constitutional rights to freedom of association would "trump" the state's generally applicable anti-discrimination policies. If not, then the consequences for religious groups that exclude legally "protected" individuals for religious reasons could be disastrous. Sincere scriptural objections to certain behaviors could be swept aside in the interest of "tolerance" and "diversity," and religious student groups could be required to conform to contemporary campus policies or be forced to disband.

Boy Scouts addressed this issue quite directly. It involved a gay former Eagle Scout's attempt to challenge the Boy Scouts' ban on gay scoutmasters. He argued that the anti-discrimination provisions of New Jersey's public accommodation law compelled the Boy Scouts to alter their policy. "Public accommodation laws" ban discrimination in "public" places. The classic public accommodation laws, for example, ban discrimination on the basis of race and sex in restaurants, hotels, and stores.

Historically, public accommodation laws were adopted for the beneficial purpose of making it possible for members of racial minorities, particularly black Americans, to travel from state to state and to be able to purchase services—hotels, restaurants, and the like—that were previously available only to white citizens. Recently, however, public accommodation laws have been used to ban discrimination even in private clubs. New Jersey's public accommodation law included a ban on discrimination on the basis of sexual orientation. Expanding public accommodation laws in order to restrict the First Amendment rights of speech and religion is a relatively new phenomenon that has become subject to considerable debate, criticism, and litigation.

In response to New Jersey's use of public accommodation law to force the Boy Scouts to alter its policies, the U.S. Supreme Court reaffirmed its commitment to freedom of association. It stated that "implicit in the right to engage in activities protected by the First Amendment is a corresponding right to associate with others in pursuit of a wide variety of political, social, economic, educational, *religious*, and cultural ends [emphasis added]." This right, the Court proclaimed, is "crucial in preventing the majority from imposing its views on groups that would rather express other, perhaps unpopular, ideas." Consequently, the Court held that the "forced inclusion of an unwanted person [in this particular case, an openly gay scout] infringes the group's free-

As a consequence of the decision in *Boy Scouts v. Dale*, a public university simply may not use its anti-discrimination policies to dictate the leadership or membership of religious organizations. If a public university allows expressive organizations to exist at all, then it must allow religious organizations to exist, to select their own leaders, and to order their own affairs.

dom of expressive association if the presence of that person affects in a significant way the group's ability to advocate public or private viewpoints."

As a consequence of the decision in *Boy Scouts v. Dale*, a public university simply may not use its anti-discrimination policies to dictate the leadership or membership of religious organizations. If a public university allows expressive organizations to exist at all, then it must allow religious organizations to exist, to select their own leaders, and to order their own affairs. Furthermore, if a private university claims that federal or state law *compels* it to coerce religious organizations to conform to such anti-discrimination policies, it is demonstrably wrong. In the words of the U.S. Supreme Court, "While the law is free to promote all sorts of conduct in place of harmful behavior, it is not free to interfere with speech for no better reason than promoting an approved message or discouraging a disfavored one, however enlightened either purpose may strike the government."

The *Boy Scouts* decision reaffirmed the U.S. Supreme Court's thinking about freedom of association and freedom of expression already expressed in *Hurley*, which had been decided five years earlier. In *Hurley*, the Supreme Court unanimously held that the private sponsors of Boston's annual St. Patrick's Day parade had a First Amendment right to exclude from the parade groups of marchers that insisted on parading with banners identifying them as gay and lesbian Irish. Such an identified group marching under its own banner would dilute—indeed, would conflict with—the conservative social and religious message that the parade sponsors meant (and had a right) to send to the world. The gay Irish group's attempt to brand the parade a "public accommodation" did not impress the Court, which ruled emphatically and without dissent that the parade was an expressive event protected by the First Amendment. Similarly, while a religious student group clearly is not free to do anything it wishes—we live, fortunately, under the rule of law—it surely has the right to define the standards and criteria of its leaders and membership, and it surely has the right to determine the message that the group will disseminate to the campus and to the world. Here, freedom of speech, religion, and association all combine very powerfully. Of course, this same principle likewise ensures a gay student group's right to define its own message by its own lights and to exclude religious fundamentalists hostile to its message from leadership positions and even from membership.

SUMMARY OF RELIGIOUS RIGHTS ON PUBLIC CAMPUSES

If a public university permits expressive organizations to exist at all, then the following basic rights belong to religious organizations on the same basis as other expressive organizations:

1) Equal access to campus facilities;
2) Equal access to university funding;
3) Freedom from university interference in the campus religious group's internal governance and composition; and
4) Basic due process of law before any rights or privileges are revoked, even for legitimate reasons. ("Due process of law" is a constitutional requirement that governments must provide individuals or organizations with notice, an opportunity to be heard, and fundamental fairness before they are deprived of "life, liberty, or property.")

Religious Liberty in the Private University

The administrators of private universities often behave as if their freedom from constitutional restrictions gives them complete discretion and free rein to restrict or destroy student liberties. They enact speech codes, they apply rules unequally, and they sometimes discriminate against religious individuals and groups at will. However, as increasing numbers of students have fought back against abuses of authority and outright oppression, private universities are beginning to understand the civic and legal realities to which they are subject. While private universities are not bound by constitutional constraints, state laws often substantially restrict their ability to engage in "Star Chamber" practices. (Courts of Star Chamber—secretive panel tribunals that violated accepted rules of fairness and acted only to protect established power—were used in Tudor England against the perceived enemies of the Crown.) Public opinion and the courts are becoming less and less inclined to put up with double standards, with disciplinary actions aimed against those who dissent from campus orthodoxy, and with the duplicity and outright fraud that have come to characterize private university judicial procedures and administrative repression.

Secular liberal arts institutions that advertise themselves as welcoming the fullest pluralism and debate too often seek to advance a particular political orthodoxy. Significantly, this agenda protects and serves the careers of college administrators, who are loathe to risk the demonstrations and bad academic publicity they fear would follow if they were to support equal freedom over favored political positions. Unlike many schools that openly declare a sectarian mission, most secular, liberal arts institutions still present themselves to the public as diverse institutions dedicated to a free exchange of ideas. They should be held to that standard. Indeed, the vulnerability of college administrators at such liberal arts institutions lies precisely in the gulf between their public self-presentation (in which they claim to support academic freedom, free speech, and the protection of individual conscience) and their practice (which all too often shows a flagrant disregard of such values). If a private college admitted in its catalogue that it was devoted to a particular established orthodoxy, and that it would assign rights unequally, it would have considerably more leeway to impose its views on the students who gave their informed consent by attending.

> At many private colleges, there is a vast gulf between their public self-presentation—in which they claim to support academic freedom, free speech, and the protection of individual conscience—and their practice—which all too often shows a flagrant disregard of such values.

Despite a tidal current of illiberal orthodoxy on the modern campus, there still is hope for civil liberties, including the indispensable right of religious liberty. Private colleges and universities may not deprive students of their legal rights in a society of law. Indeed, legal doctrines long reserved for more traditional commercial arrangements now have new applicability to the campus setting, and they may be used on behalf of the rights of belief and conscience. The suppression of religious expression and association can be ended not only by the requirements of fair process and good faith, but also, indeed, by the ancient and enduring maxims of civilized contract law.

To prevail in the battle for religious liberty, besieged members of a private university community must understand and apply several appropriate legal doctrines. These doctrines, as noted, can vary from state to state, but enough common principles exist to provide some general guidance. For those who treasure liberty, the law can still provide a refuge (although, as we shall see, publicity may sometimes be a more effective and powerful tool, because university administrators are hard pressed to admit and justify publicly the private basis of their actions). The strength of that legal refuge depends on multiple factors—the laws of the individual state in which the university is located; the content of university catalogues, handbooks, and disciplinary rules; and the precise governance and funding of the institution.

INDIVIDUAL STATE LAWS AFFECTING
PRIVATE INSTITUTIONS

In America's federalist structure, the states have remarkably diverse legal systems. Rights can vary tremendously from state to state. However, the U.S. Constitution limits the extent to which any state may regulate the private universities in their midst, since the Bill of Rights (which applies both to the states and to the federal government) protects private institutions from excessive government interference. In particular, the First Amendment protects the academic freedom of colleges and universities at least as much as (and frequently more than) it protects the individuals at those institutions.

Decent societies have historically found ways to protect individuals from indecent behavior. State law often reflects that tradition of decency, and it is particularly relevant to how a university applies its policies and to how university officials behave toward students (and faculty). For example, some states have formulated common-law rules for associations—which include private universities—that prohibit "arbitrary or capricious" decision-making and that require organizations, at an absolute minimum, *to follow their own rules* and to deal in good faith with their members. These standards can be profoundly valuable defenses of liberty in the politically supercharged environment of the modern campus, where discipline without notice or hearing is commonplace.

> Because states have diverse legal systems, your rights can vary dramatically from state to state. In general, however, states will protect individuals from *fraud* and other types of *misrepresentation*.

It is not uncommon for students or groups that deviate from campus orthodoxy to be essentially "railroaded" off campus. Campus officials or judicial courts might hold closed, late-night meetings; they might not inform accused students or groups of the charges against them; they might not offer protection from threats and intimidation to "offensive" students holding poorly understood religious views. It may also be the case that, while several other individuals have committed the same offense, or other groups have the same policies, religious groups are the only ones to be prosecuted. In such cases, they may be able to force the university literally to take a step back and to begin to employ sound procedures in a fair way. Good faith requires fair process and often prohibits extremes of arbitrary decision-making.

State law also provides common-law rules against *mis - representation*. Simply put, there is a long tradition of laws against fraud and deceit. Very often, a university's recruiting materials, brochures, and even its "admitted student" orientations—which are designed to entice individuals to attend that institution rather than another—will trumpet a school's commitment to "diversity," "inclusion," and "tolerance." Sometimes religious students will be personally assured that they will find a "home" or be "welcome" in the campus community. Promises such as these will often induce religious students to bypass opportunities (and even scholarships) at other schools and to enroll in the private secular university. If these promises of "tolerance" or of a place in the community later turn out to be demonstrably false, a university could find itself in serious legal jeopardy.

There are legal doctrines with strange-sounding names, such as "promissory estoppel," "detrimental reliance," and "fraudulent inducement," that prevent real abuses, such as depriving an individual of the promised rights and goods on which he or she relied in accepting someone's offer. If a university promises religious liberty and legal equality, and individuals rely on that promise, causing them to pass up other opportunities, the university may not walk away from its inducement. A university has no right to let a student make a decision based on its enticements and then renege on its obligations. To say the least, it may not promise religious liberty and then put someone on trial for exercising it. Private universities may rightfully be beyond the reach of the Constitution, but they have no license to deceive with false promises. In short, prohibitions against fraudulent inducement to contract and against false advertising can be used to force a change in an administration's behavior. Furthermore, such prohibitions can also be a source of substantial monetary damages for the wronged student, a legal fact that can in turn be used to motivate administrators to protect the rights and dignity of all students equally.

When applying to a college or university, students should ask for its specific policies on religious liberty, nondiscrimination on the basis of religion (including the lack of religion), and legal equality. Individuals already at an institution who find themselves and their religious organization subjected to disciplinary action should immediately look very closely at university promotional materials, brochures, and websites. They should also attempt to recollect (and to confirm with others) any specific conversations they may have had with university officials regarding their religious liberty. If those promises or inducements are clear enough, then a court may very well hold the university to its word. This is an area of the law, however, with many, many variations. Some courts have given colleges vast leeway in interpreting and following their own internal policies and promises; thus, in some states, a college will be held only to "general"—as opposed to "strict"—adherence to its own rules. In general, though, most state judicial systems insist that a college not ignore its own guidelines and promises, and almost every state offers serious protection from outright fraud. Also, the public does not respect fraudulent behavior or institutional double standards. If a college or university changes its rules in order to discriminate against religion, its subsequent use of double standards will not, as a matter of law, violate its regulations or promises. Its behavior and motives, however, will become obvious to everyone, which likely would cause public disapproval, diminished enrollment, and reduced donations.

It is very common for religious individuals who dissent from the campus orthodoxy concerning Scripture and sexuality to be the victims of hate campaigns and verbal abuse. Of course, just as religious students should have the right to bear witness to their beliefs, it is the right of the critics of such religious students to express their views and to bear their own moral witness. The crucial issue here is that the same rules should apply equally to all. For example, during an incident at Tufts University, various student organizations covered the campus with anti-Christian graffiti and hurled terms of abuse at religious minorities. They told demonstrable falsehoods about the Tufts Christian Fellowship ("TCF"), an evangelical Christian student group. If the members of the TCF had engaged in similar behavior against its attackers, the judicial wrath of the University would have fallen upon them with a vengeance. For example, the TCF might be charged with "homophobia" for its sincere religious belief that homosexual acts are sinful, but critics of the TCF never would be charged with anti-Christian bigotry. At Tufts, only one group was expected to change its beliefs and to change the lawful behaviors that follow from those beliefs. Such a double standard violates all promises of legal equality, nondiscrimination on the basis of creed, and religious liberty.

While the law does not protect either minority religions or minority lifestyles from harmful statements of opinion, it does protect individuals from certain kinds of demonstrably false assertions and accusations. State laws prohibit libel, slander, and defamation (although too many of us confuse hurtful opinion with these torts). Further, if a hate campaign turns truly vicious—involving, for example, physical intimidation, threats of violence, harassing phone calls, and improper inquiries into confidential information—one indeed may be the victim of impermissible and punishable acts. Everyone has legal protection from unlawful terrorist threats, intentional infliction of emotional distress, invasion of privacy, or actual harassment. Again, in all of these matters, the rights and protections of religious students, in circumstances of promised legal equality, should be the same as those of all others.

THE ROLE OF UNIVERSITY CATALOGUES, HANDBOOKS, AND DISCIPLINARY RULES

Ironically, the very universities that persecute religious minorities may also be their best source of protection. The reason for this is simple and revealing: most private, secular universities make broad and glowing statements about the protected rights of their own students. They have chosen to describe themselves to the world as decent institutions dedicated to fairness, the search for truth, tolerance, and legal equality.

A private university student's best protection against persecution and abuse is often the university's own written policies.

Many of the catalogues, student handbooks, and disciplinary codes of private universities promise non-discrimination on the basis of religion, freedom of speech and association, and a judicial system with fair hearings prior to any disciplinary action. While it is a source of considerable aggravation for many students to observe the rank hypocrisy of colleges and universities that make and then ignore such self-presentations, these public assurances nonetheless provide ample opportunity for forcing colleges and universities to follow the principles that they advertise and preach.

Most state courts hold that the contents of university catalogues and handbooks constitute, at least to some degree, *contracts* between the university and its students. Consequently, if a university has stated a policy in writing, a court will require the university to adhere to that policy.

As a general rule, *if a university has stated a policy in writing, a court will require the university to adhere to that policy.* Most state courts hold that the contents of university catalogues and handbooks constitute, at least to some degree, contracts between the university and its students. While some state courts have held that the university and its students are not in a contractual relationship, most of them use other legal theories to require universities to comply with the terms of their own documents. Often, a court perceives an inequality in bargaining power between the university (which drew up the contract) and the student, and it will resolve ambiguities in the language of the publications in favor of the student.

Unfortunately, the contents of these publications are rapidly changing, often upon the advice of lawyers paid to reduce a college's exposure to liability from lawsuits (rather than help the colleges live up to their historic obligations to academic freedom and the rights of conscience). Instead of providing blanket free speech rights to their students, universities now improvise speech codes, usually found in the "verbal conduct" or "verbal behavior" sections of harassment policies. Furthermore, instead of providing students with fair hearings, universities increasingly hold secret proceedings. However, even the most outwardly repressive universities can provide their students with a surprising number of rights, because even the cleverest lawyers have difficulty wiping out from a college catalogue all of the high phrases about liberty and fairness that colleges like to use to present themselves to the world.

The recent Tufts University incident presents an excellent example of how handbooks can affect and protect students, even at universities with selective and politically motivated harassment and anti-discrimination policies. At Tufts, the Tufts Christian Fellowship was derecognized (essentially banned) after it refused to permit an openly lesbian student to lead the group. The derecognition decision was made—without notice to the TCF—by the tribunal of the Student Judiciary at a secret, late-night meeting.

Tufts' student handbook stated that it was university policy not to discriminate on the basis of religion. It also stated that Tufts respected the freedom of association. It added, however, that student organizations were not allowed to discriminate on the basis of, among other things, religion and sexual orientation. Tufts was remarkably unaware of the profound conflict among these various principles. It is simply impossible for a university to respect freedom of association and religious liberty while simultaneously prohibiting religious groups from using religious criteria as a basis for selecting members, let alone leaders.

Although the handbooks were confusing about the true extent of the TCF's religious liberties, it was clear enough that the Student Judiciary's secret, late-night meeting violated the TCF's rights to fair process. The student handbooks provided for at least two sets of open hearings, in front of impartial tribunals, before any student organization could be punished for violating school rules. Once Tufts was reeling from FIRE's public exposure of the case, the University acknowledged its wrong when a University appeals panel reversed the Student

Judiciary's decision and re-recognized the TCF. At later hearings, the TCF's ability to cite its rights as set forth in Tufts' handbooks prevented a host of further injustices and proved instrumental in securing the TCF's eventual victory.

Thus, if students find themselves or their organi-

> As the Tufts incident illustrates, even if university policy is ambiguous or unfavorable, disciplinary codes will often provide for *open hearings* that allow religious students and groups to state their case.

zation facing university discipline, or if they find that their university is trying to impose new or discriminatory policies on them, it is absolutely *critical* that they read *every word* of the university's handbooks and catalogues. Indeed, students should not stop with these documents. They should search the school's website thoroughly and pick up copies of its admissions materials. Many courts will be sympathetic to the argument that students' tens of thousands of tuition dollars buy them not just an education but also a school's good faith adherence to its written policies. Even if administrators don't realize the importance of following the rules, their lawyers almost certainly will. If not, then most judges will.

THE ROLE OF UNIVERSITY GOVERNANCE AND FUNDING

A final source of possible legal protection for a student at a private university might be found in a particularly difficult legal and political area, namely, the extent of the government's involvement in the financing and governance of a school. If that involvement goes beyond a certain point, it is possible that the school will be deemed, for legal purposes, "public," and in that case, all consti-

> On occasion, colleges that advertise themselves as private are—because of excessive government funding or governmental control—actually public.

tutional protections will apply. This happened, for example, at the University of Pittsburgh and at Temple University, both in Pennsylvania. State laws there require that, in return for significant public funding, a certain number of state offi-

cials must serve on the schools' boards. That fact led these formerly "private" universities to be treated, legally, as "public." In fact, however, this is a very rare occurrence, and the odds of any private school being deemed legally public are very slim, indeed. Unless a school is officially public, one always should assume that the First Amendment does not apply there.

There are many students, faculty members, and even lawyers who believe, wholly erroneously, that if a college receives *any* federal or state funding, it is therefore "public." In fact, accepting governmental funds usually makes the university subject *only* to the conditions—sometimes broad, sometimes narrow—explicitly attached to those specific funds. (The two most prominent conditions attached to all federal funding are nondiscrimination on the basis of race and gender.) Furthermore, the "strings" attached to virtually all federal grants are not always helpful to the cause of liberty. This is one reason why people who worry about excessive government power can be opposed to governmental funding of private colleges and universities.

As a legal matter, there is no specific level of federal funding that obligates a private college or institution to honor the First Amendment. Many factors, such as university governance, the appointment of trustees, and specific acts of legislation, need to be weighed in determining the status of any given institution. That should not stop students, however, from learning as much as they can about the funding and governance of their institution. Do the taxpayers truly want to subsidize assaults upon religious liberty? Do members of the Board of Trustees truly want to be party to such assaults? Do donors want to pay for an attack on a right that most Americans hold so dear? Information

Although private schools rarely become public through excessive government funding or control, knowledge about funding and control can enable students to alert various institutions (legislatures, alumni, charitable foundations) that can exert real influence over even private university administrations.

57

about funding and governance is vital and useful. For example, students may find that a major foundation is a substantial source of funds contributed to their college, and they may undertake to contact that foundation to report on how the university selectively abuses the rights and consciences of students of faith. Colleges are *extremely* sensitive to contributors learning about official bigotry and injustice at the institutions they support.

SUMMARY OF RELIGIOUS RIGHTS ON PRIVATE CAMPUSES

Because private colleges have such broad freedom to determine their own policies and because state laws vary so widely, it is best, as a matter of law, to speak only of having "potential" rights on a private campus. However, the following generalizations can be made with a certain degree of confidence, unless you have given informed consent to be part of a voluntary association in which you have waived these rights:

1) You have the right to rational, nonarbitrary disciplinary proceedings and, to a lesser extent, to rational, nonarbitrary results;

2) You have the right to receive treatment equal to that received by those who have engaged in similar behavior;

3) You have the right to honesty and good faith from university officials; and

4) You have the right to enjoy all of the rights promised you by university catalogues, handbooks, and disciplinary codes.

IDENTIFYING THREATS TO RELIGIOUS LIBERTY

The Tactics of Oppression

The methods of attacking religious liberty are limited only by the creativity of the oppressors. When guardians of the new orthodoxy sense threats to their campus power and rule, they often will use whatever means are available to them to purge, silence, or punish the "heretic."

Sometimes the attacks on your beliefs and practices will come merely through ridicule and attempts at public humiliation, and you should not confuse these attacks, if they use lawful means, with assaults upon your liberty. Often, liberty means that you will need the courage to bear witness to your faith and conscience. Other individuals have the same rights of private and public expression that you have (but they should not have more than you do). Freedom for you means freedom for all.

> *"The quality and creative power of student intellectual life to this day remains a vital measure of a school's influence and attainment. For the University, by regulation, to cast disapproval on particular viewpoints of its students risks the suppression of free speech and creative inquiry in one of the vital centers for the Nation's intellectual life, its college and university campuses."*
>
> JUSTICE ANTHONY KENNEDY
> *Rosenberger v. University of Virginia (1995)*

At other times, however, there will be a formal assault upon your religious liberty and your rights of conscience, with campus power using university "rules" and "courts" in an effort to eliminate the influence or presence of religious students and groups whose beliefs and creeds others find "offensive." Sadly, experience teaches that religious individuals and organizations are most often victimized by university policies that, in theory, were enacted to *promote* tolerance, diversity, and fairness. These are 1) anti-discrimination policies; 2) speech codes; and 3) harassment codes.

The Use of Anti-discrimination Policies

Many if not most campuses have adopted comprehensive anti-discrimination policies. These policies apply not only to hiring, admissions, and academic policies, but also to student life. Often, student organizations will be instructed to adhere to policies that prohibit discrimination on the basis of "race, religion, gender, ethnicity, nationality, disability, sexual orientation, or marital status." Anti-discrimination policies are introduced and taught at mandatory student orientations that effectively coerce students into re-examining long-held beliefs. Often, student organizations are required to submit constitutions or other documents that contain promises to abide by university anti-discrimination policies. In fact, fidelity to these policies is often a prerequisite to enjoying any university benefit. The anti-discrimination policy is the "loyalty oath" of the modern academy.

Religious individuals and groups are most often accused of violating anti-discrimination policies relating to gender, sexuality, and religion. As noted, several campus religious organizations are under attack because they allegedly have "discriminated" by using religion, religious doctrine, and religious belief as criteria in choosing their members or leaders.

> Anti-discrimination codes should not be used to limit the freedom of religious individuals and organizations to make religiously motivated decisions or to engage in religious speech.

A moment's thought will reveal both the extraordinary threat to religious liberty and the utter wrongheadedness of using "anti-discrimination" policies to discriminate against religious belief. The assault upon the liberty of a religious group usually begins when a student member of a religious organization or, indeed, a student outside the organization feels discriminated against by a religious organization or individual. Perhaps the offended student was rejected for a leadership position in the group on the basis of theological disagreements (such as disagreements about virtuous and sinful behavior). Perhaps the student simply believes that the presence of such religious groups contributes to an "atmosphere of intolerance" on campus.

> Students who are offended by religious speech and conduct often claim that religious students have discriminated against them or others who share the offended student's race, gender, or sexual orientation.

Often, students are offended simply by the idea that "fundamentalists" and "traditionalists" are gathered in their midst. On today's campuses, people of faith are widely viewed as uniquely intolerant because of their theological beliefs about such issues as gender roles, abortion, and sexual practices.

Whatever the reason for the initial complaint, once that complaint is made, religious groups often find themselves waging a difficult, lonely, and defensive struggle. The student or group filing a complaint is often termed a "victim," so the accused find themselves as "victimizers," confronting informal charges of bigotry and formal charges of discrimination. Frequently, the very students, faculty, and administrators who will be judging the validity of the complaint are participating in protests against the religious group. (Keep track of such a thing: it is a clear violation of any promise of an impartial and unbiased hearing.) When faced with name-calling, an intimidating atmosphere, or formal charges, many religious groups simply collapse and cave in to campus pressure. Rather than fight for their religious liberty, many individuals and groups surrender and submit to historically unprecedented administrative interference in purely religious decisions, abandoning their witness to their deep convictions and to religious traditions that have stood for millennia.

If religious groups continue to abandon their principles and living beliefs in response to accusations of "discrimination," they will find that they are no longer autonomous—self-governing by their own consciences—in any meaningful sense. Each group will be at the mercy of the most easily offended individual at their institution. Religious groups—defined as broadly as the U.S. Supreme Court has defined them—must draw a line of conscience and conviction in the sand. Students at public universities, believers and unbelievers alike, must emphatically assert their rights to freedom of religion, conscience, association, and speech. Students at private universities should use every protection of common law, contract, and public exposure at their disposal. To the fullest extent possible, religious students must not allow their persecutors to frame the terms of the debate. Even if the other side initiates the charge, students of faith should restate it in their own honest terms: The issue is *not* whether this or that group should be "protected" from "religious intolerance." The issue is whether we preserve or extinguish religious liberty and religious pluralism. The issue is whether a campus can overcome its own political orthodoxy and tolerate the religious traditions of others. In other words, the issue is: Will the university permit *you* to follow the dictates of *your* conscience when you are neither interfering with the legitimate rights of others nor threatening their health or safety? In that context, it is crucial to understand that the "legitimate rights of others" do not include the "right" not to be offended or excluded by the membership criteria, beliefs, and activities of a religious group. There is no such "right." Instead, each student has a right to believe, to practice his beliefs, and to associate with others who are willing to associate with

> In response to discrimination charges, do not allow yourself or your religious group to be branded as "intolerant" or "discriminatory." The issue is *not* whether this or that group should be "protected" from "religious intolerance." The issue is whether we preserve or extinguish religious liberty and religious pluralism.

him or her. No one has a "right" to force himself or herself into another's expressive or religious group.

In 1943, the Supreme Court issued one of its most powerful and eloquent decisions—a decision that is as meaningful today as it was almost sixty years ago. In the case of *West Virginia Board of Education v. Barnette*, the Court ruled that the state of West Virginia could not require all children to salute the American flag. Several students believed the flag salute was an act of idolatry forbidden by Scripture. For the modern American college student, school anti-discrimination requirements constitute a "pledge to diversity" in the same way that the pledge to the flag is a "pledge to Americanism." In the Court's majority opinion, Justice Robert Jackson condemned the flag salute requirement because it compelled a student "to declare a belief ...[and] to utter what is not on [his or her] mind." In some of the most famous words ever written by a justice of the Supreme Court, Justice Jackson wrote: "If there is any fixed star in our constitutional constellation, it is that no official, high or petty, can prescribe what will be orthodox, in politics, nationalism, religion, or matters of opinion or force citizens to confess by word or act their faith [in it]." For the public school administrator, those words are law. For the private school administrator, those words represent our national conscience and ideal. They ignore them at their peril.

Dramatically, *Barnette* was decided during World

War II, when there was a social premium placed on patriotic activities such as the pledge to the flag. If the Supreme Court could insist that even during such a time a Jehovah's Witness child could not be forced to raise his arm and pledge to the flag, then surely no university administration is within its rights to insist that religious students pledge fidelity to a definition of "diversity" that would undermine their religious beliefs. True diversity is achieved by making the campus safe for an authentic multiplicity of religious, secular, conservative, liberal, traditionalist, and radical groups alike.

Colleges often attempt to justify expansive anti-discrimination policies by stating that those policies are "required by law." In reality, these policies often violate the law. No state law or federal statute takes precedence over the Constitution, period. Not even a private university can truthfully claim that state laws compel it to enact policies that violate your religious liberties. When confronted by anti-discrimination policies, remember *Barnette*. A public university cannot "prescribe what will

Colleges often attempt to justify anti-discrimination policies by stating that those policies are "required by law." However, no state law or federal statute takes precedence over the Constitution, period. Not even a private university can truthfully claim that state laws compel it to enact policies that violate your religious liberties.

be orthodox" in your and your group's faith. A private university is never required to do so, and if it chooses to prescribe a new orthodoxy, then it chooses the path of repression.

The Use of Speech Codes

There are now many campuses that have either inherently oppressive speech codes, or, more commonly, politically biased speech codes that are enforced and sustained by double standards. (Who has ever been tried for "offending" a Catholic or Buddhist or an evangelical Christian?) On such campuses, every religious individual or person of conscience risks prosecution.

Though almost never used by colleges and universities themselves, "speech code" is the appropriate name for such repressive policies. In a public university, a speech code will almost never meet constitutional standards, and punishment of a religious individual for a violation should rarely last longer than the time it takes for a lawyer to write a letter or make a phone call. FIRE is aware of no authentic speech code at a public university that has survived judicial attack.

> *Speech code* is the common term for university regulations that punish speech that the university (or others) find harmful or offensive.

Recall, however, that private colleges and universities do not have to respect constitutional free speech rights, and few of them do. The best legal and tactical response in these circumstances, therefore, is to ensure that proper disciplinary procedures are followed. If cases receive open hearings or true public scrutiny, the absurdity of the underlying charge can be exposed. Exposure in turn often leads universities to back away from their charges. Even if campus administrators are not initially swayed, the weight of alumni and public opinion can often be brought to bear on your behalf. Speech codes are singularly unpopular in the wider world; people across the political spectrum oppose them, and alumni generally despise them. Letter writing campaigns and press releases to members of the media sympathetic to freedom of speech, freedom of conscience, and religious liberty often can result in changed campus minds. This is a country that truly believes in religious pluralism, and you can use that moral reality to benefit your cause. Remember always to focus on the heart of the issue: the university's abusive intolerance of your beliefs and its double standard in applying its rules.

Liberal arts institutions invariably promise academic freedom, the rights of individual conscience, and respect for each individual's search for truth. Because of that, as noted, speech codes are often in flagrant conflict with such assurances and can thus be attacked, in court if necessary, as violations of the institution's contract with its students. Administrators are hard pressed to defend publicly their obvious selective double standards and hypocrisies. The real sensitivity of colleges and universities to public opinion makes media exposure a powerful weapon against speech codes.

> Speech codes at public universities are almost always unconstitutional. At private universities, they tend to be both unpopular and incompatible with basic notions of academic freedom.

The Use of Harassment Codes

Because the phrase "speech code" so clearly signifies oppression and an assault on academic freedom, the term has become rare in higher education, both public and private. Many professors lost their jobs in the 1950s because of assaults upon free speech, and many students were expelled in the 1960s for the exercise of their rights of free expression. As a new generation of speech codes began to appear in the 1980s and were tested in court, however, it became obvious that, at public universities at least, they were not going to pass constitutional scrutiny. Private universities, while not subject to First Amendment limitations, were often embarrassed to find themselves in the position of seeming to offer their students fewer speech rights than were available for students at public institutions. Indeed, a university's admission that it had a "speech code" often proved shameful because the very term seemed so obviously incompatible with academic freedom. Thus, campuses began to change not their repressive behaviors but the names they gave them. "Speech codes" increasingly were replaced by "harassment codes." Who, after all, could object to a code that forbade one student to harass another? Just as "speech codes" had become an embarrassment, federal legislation and regulation began to take aim at sexual harassment, a phrase

> University prohibitions against harassment should not be used as disguised speech codes.

that has now become ubiquitous. Harassment codes initially arose from the common-sense recognition in federal law that it was inconsistent to end job discrimination but to permit hostile conditions that made it impossible for someone actually to work.

All universities prohibit sexual harassment—words or conduct that create a "hostile environment" on the basis of sex—and many also prohibit racial or religious harassment. Many of these policies are quite straightforward and reflect simply the requirements of federal and state law (requirements that never, of course, can violate the Constitution or the Bill of Rights). Other policies, however, especially (but not solely) at private colleges and universities, go far beyond the requirements of law and permit or, indeed, require that any words or conduct *that are subjectively offensive to a member of a protected class* be treated as punishable harassment. In other words, if a person feels harassed, then, in the university's eyes, that person *is* harassed.

> Harassment regulations should not be used to prohibit any words or conduct that merely are *subjectively* offensive to a member of a protected class.

An example of the kind of harassment charges that religious individuals can face happened recently at Cornell University. In the midst of campus debate about campus gay rights policies and ordinances, a Christian professor posted some material opposing the proposed gay rights policy and outlining an orthodox Christian position on homosexual behavior. Rather than engaging him in any kind of substantive debate (or simply ignoring him), several students charged him with sexual harassment. The professor not only became a pariah on campus but he was summoned to official hearings and faced charges that placed his job and career in jeopardy. It was only after the intervention of a legal foundation devoted to religious liberty that such extraordinary charges were dropped and his career preserved.

For the public school student, the Constitution provides almost absolute protection from the kind of harassment charges faced by the Cornell professor. In fact, a federal Court of Appeals, in the case of *Saxe v. State*

College Area School District (2001), recently struck down a high school anti-harassment policy that—like many university policies—prohibited "verbal or physical conduct based on… race, religion, color, national origin, gender, sexual orientation, disability, or other personal characteristics, and which has the purpose or effect of substantially interfering with a student's educational performance or creating an intimidating, hostile or offensive environment." (This language, by the way, is found everywhere in harassment codes on and off campus, and is commonly called the "hostile environment" clause. From a First Amendment point of view, it is vital to understand that the First Amendment protects speech even if someone subjectively decides that another person's expression creates a "hostile environment." Some behaviors indeed may be outlawed as true harassment, but causing discomfort by the mere expression of belief falls under the category of constitutionally protected speech.)

> At *public universities*, the Constitution protects individuals or groups from being punished for speech that is merely offensive to a person or group.

In *Saxe*, the Court found that the school district's broad policy, which prevented students from making negative comments about other students' appearance, clothing, social skills, and even values, "strikes at the heart of moral and political discourse—the lifeblood of

constitutional self-government (and democratic education) and the core concern of the First Amendment." In
the Court's words, the fact that some speech may offend
"is not a cause for its prohibition, but rather the reason
for its protection." Simply put, the government cannot
prevent you from sharing your religious views just
because some students may find those views offensive.

For the private school student, the situation is, again,
more complex. You should be extremely familiar with
stated school policy on stu-
dents' rights to an open
hearing, and you should
know whether your school
explicitly promises to protect religious belief and
expression. Ironically, the
policies of many schools
may prohibit religious
harassment to the same
extent that they prohibit
sexual harassment. Anti-
religious students some-
times use far more offensive
language to describe you

> *Private school* students should
> attack unfair anti-harassment
> regulations in the same way
> that they do speech codes—
> by seeking to apply public
> pressure and by using, to
> maximum advantage, other
> school policies, such as
> guarantees of academic
> freedom and the right to a
> public hearing.

than you used to "harass" your "victim." In such a situation, filing a harassment counterclaim can bring the
whole proceeding to a crashing halt. Faced with the
prospect of censoring anti-religious expression, colleges

and universities usually rediscover free speech and the desirability of open debate.

There is perhaps a certain bizarre logic in the campus argument that an orthodox Muslim, Christian, Jewish, or other religious student who expresses religiously based criticisms of premarital sex, homosexual conduct, contemporary gender roles, or abortion is thereby "harassing" students with different beliefs or practices. The legal definition of harassment, however, is quite different from what prevails in today's campus codes. Traditionally, "harassment" applied merely to speech has meant speech delivered in a time, place, or manner intended to disturb rather than to communicate. Thus, telephoning someone at three o'clock every morning to say "I hate you" is harassment because of the disturbing time and manner of delivery. Such conduct would also be harassment even if the message were "I love you," unless the listener invited the message and the timing. If someone calls a religious person a "born-again bigot," for example, that is the expression of an opinion, and intolerance is no crime. If someone awakened a religious student every night to say, "I agree with you," preventing him from working or sleeping, that indeed could be harassment.

It is not, for example, harassment for a Catholic group to argue vociferously that abortion is murder. While such an assertion doubtless would be seen as offensive or hostile by pro-choice individuals, or by women who have had an abortion and do not like to be called "murderers of innocent life," Catholics who express such beliefs are fully protected. It would be wholly different, however, if the Catholic group continually phoned a woman and whispered "murderer" into the phone, preventing her from working, or sleeping, or enjoying a certain peace. The problem, in short, is that many college administrators and students consider speech and expression that upsets a politically favored student in any way to be "harassment." In this respect, "harassment" codes are simply "offensive speech codes" in disguise.

Despite the change of name, then, nothing has changed since the days of openly named speech codes. When religious students are charged with "harassment" for expressing and practicing their beliefs, they can often defend themselves simply by clarifying the muddled thinking of their opponents. Making an analogy on the basis of legal equality (ask, for example, if it is "harassment" when pro-choice activists offend pro-life Catholics by their actions or expressions) is often an instructive and effective argument.

FIVE STEPS TO FIGHTING BACK

When faced with an attack on your religious liberty:

1. Take careful notes of conversations and keep copies of any written correspondence with university officials, whether administrators, faculty members, or student leaders;

2. *Carefully* read your student handbook, disciplinary code, and other policies applicable to you or your organization;

3. Reread the sections of this guide that are applicable to your school—public or private;

4. Build a coalition—contact other students or student groups that may suffer from the same policies or action;

5. Call FIRE.

When you are empowered with the knowledge contained in this guide, armed with the information applicable to your unique situation, and allied with the committed advocates at FIRE, you will no longer be helpless or alone. Time and again, courageous students who have followed these precise steps have turned the tide against religious persecution and restored true diversity to their university communities.

CONCLUSION:
FIGHTING BACK

It is easy for persecuted individuals and groups to feel alone. It is extremely rare for a persecuted student to be a part of a religious majority on campus or to be perceived as part of the mainstream of campus life. University officials often feel free to attack religious individuals precisely because such students (or faculty) often have little or no campus support.

This feeling of isolation is compounded when the persecuted individual is instructed repeatedly to keep the dispute "in the community," as if universities were somehow sacrosanct entities that would be corrupted by the knowledge and outrage of "outsiders." Many southern sheriffs defending segregation used to talk that way in the 1950s. The pressure to stay silent is reinforced by "secret" meetings and "confidential," "informal" contacts. Administrators indicate to accused students that they will receive reasonable treatment if they agree to campus "dialogue" (a code word for what totalitarians call "thought reform" and "re-education"). The power of vocal anti-religious campus activists also serves to convince religious students that any extra attention to their problem will only cause them more harm. If the world is against them, why invite more of the world into the dispute?

Although it requires no small amount of courage to bear moral witness, you should never acquiesce to demands to "keep quiet" or to disingenuous pressure to "resolve" things "within the community." Your freedom is the foundation of everyone else's freedom, whether they know that or not. It is malicious for campus officials to bring charges against isolated religious individuals or groups and then reinforce their isolation by insisting that they cut off their access to outside assistance. This malice is also a mark of weakness, because it arises ultimately from fear. It is rare, indeed, for oppressors to survive the glare of publicity unscathed, especially in a nation as devoted to religious liberty and religious pluralism as America historically has been. To say the least, you are *not* alone.

In the long run, there are many individuals and groups beyond the walls of your campus who will support your rights passionately and vigorously. This large group includes many, many people who may disagree thoroughly with your religious beliefs, but who will never-

> *"Both morals and sound policy require that the state should not violate the conscience of the individual. . . . So deep in its significance and vital, indeed, is it to the integrity of man's moral and spiritual nature that nothing short of self-preservation of the state should warrant its violation; and it may well be questioned whether the state which preserves its life by a settled policy of violation of the conscience of the individual will not in fact ultimately lose it by the process."*
>
> CHIEF JUSTICE HARLAN FISKE STONE
> *"The Conscientious Objector," (1919)*

theless defend your crucial right to express your views and to live by the lights of your conscience without being charged with harassment. Such supporters will need to know, of course, that the time, place, and manner of your religious expression did not interfere with the rights and safety of others. If they know that you truly are being prosecuted for the content of your beliefs, they will not be indifferent. They will understand far more than campus zealots could ever imagine that it is *not* a violation of the rights and safety of others to express or bear witness to something that others merely find unpleasant, offensive, or psychologically uncomfortable.

Realize that while political orthodoxies may seem to rule unchallenged at your institutions, they do not govern mainstream American life. This is a nation that truly values religious liberty and individual rights. Campus oppressors, when forced to explain their actions to the press, to alumni, or to judges, look foolish, hypocritical, and more concerned with advancing their academic careers than with protecting the essential freedoms of their students and faculty.

Realize, too, that you cannot delegate your fight for freedom to like-minded faculty members. If you want to protect your rights, then you must act. Recent court decisions have resulted in *less* academic freedom for professors and administrators. Students generally possess more free speech rights and religious liberties than any other person or entity on campus, and therefore it is students who must take the lead in protecting those freedoms. The reason that students are generally freer than professors is that they are legally *customers* of the college, while professors are its employees. As in any business, an employer has considerable latitude to establish working rules for its employees, although academic employees are protected to some considerable extent by academic freedom. Students, however, enjoy greater leeway. A store may instruct its clerks to greet customers with "Good morning" and may punish them for not complying. It may not deal in a similar manner, to say the least, with its customers.

When you defend your liberty, you will not fight alone. In the words of the late Supreme Court Justice Louis Brandeis: "Sunlight is the best disinfectant." Campus oppressors cannot justify in the light of day

what they do to students within what FIRE's co-
founders, Alan Charles Kors and Harvey A. Silverglate,
term "The Shadow University." The Foundation for
Individual Rights in Education exists to bring oppression
to light, and, once it has been exposed, to destroy it. To
that end, FIRE sustains a formidable array of media contacts, academic relationships, and legal allies across the
broadest spectrum of opinion, all of whom are committed to individual rights. Persecuted members of the academic community—even if they are completely isolated
on campus—should not feel alone. Since 1999, FIRE has
deployed its resources on behalf of individual students,
faculty members, and student groups at schools small
and large, public and private. If your individual rights are
being trampled, visit www.thefire.org. FIRE will defend
you, and, in similar circumstances, it will defend the real
rights of your critics. Liberty and legal equality are not
merely for this or that individual or group. They are a
way of being human that leaves us capable, within the
law, of moral choice and personal responsibility.
Religious liberty, as the world has learned, is one of the
most vital aspects of human freedom and dignity.

The struggle for campus religious liberties has truly
begun. After almost four decades of retreat, religious
individuals are beginning to draw their own rightful lines
and to make their own stands at universities across the
country. The stakes could not be higher for those who
treasure free expression, who value true diversity, and

who understand that the right to private conscience is the most fundamental and irreducible of liberties. Those of you who have experienced efforts to repress your thoughts, convictions, and souls now must take a stand on behalf of your foundational rights as human beings. For too long, the guardians of campus orthodoxy have been permitted to twist the meanings of "tolerance" and "inclusion," denying both to persons of faith. It is time to name and resist campus leaders who tolerate only those who bow before their chosen gods and who include only those who worship at their particular ideological shrines.

It is no exaggeration to say that the future of American freedom is at stake in the struggle for campus liberty and legal equality. America's students cannot learn to respect freedom if they participate in—or passively tolerate—tyranny. Today's college campus is tomorrow's public, political, educational, and civic culture. By standing against campus persecution, by fighting the tyranny of enforced orthodoxy and legal inequality, religious individuals and their supporters preserve not only their own consciences, but also the liberty of our entire society.

CASE APPENDIX

The following cases were each discussed in the text of the guide. Their precise legal citations are below. The cases are listed in their order of appearance.

Cantwell v. Connecticut, 310 U.S. 296 (1940).

Zelman v. Simmons-Harris, 122 S. Ct. 2460 (2002).

Sherbert v. Verner, 374 U.S. 398 (1963).

Employment Division v. Smith, 494 U.S. 872 (1990).

Church of the Lukumi Babalu Aye, Inc. v. Hialeah, 508 U.S. 520 (1993).

United States v. Seeger, 380 U.S. 163 (1965).

Welsh v. United States, 398 U.S. 333 (1970).

Torcaso v. Watkins, 367 U.S. 488 (1961).

Frazee v. Illinois Department of Employment Security, 489 U.S. 829 (1989).

Thomas v. Review Board of Indiana Employment Security Division, 450 U.S. 707 (1981).

Rosenberger v. University of Virginia, 515 U.S. 819 (1995).

West Virginia Board of Education v. Barnette, 319 U.S. 624 (1943).

Saxe v. State College Area School District, 240 F.3d 200 (2001).

Widmar v. Vincent, 454 U.S. 263 (1981).

Lamb's Chapel v. Center Moriches Union Free School, 508 U.S. 384 (1993).

Good News Club v. Milford Central School, 121 S.Ct. 2093 (2001).

University of Wisconsin v. Southworth, 529 U.S. 217 (2000).

Hurley v. Irish-American Gay, Lesbian and Bisexual Group of Boston, 515 U.S. 557 (1995).

Boy Scouts of America v. Dale, 530 U.S. 640 (2000).

87

Alan Dershowitz – Alan Dershowitz is the Felix Frankfurter Professor of Law at the Harvard Law School. He is an expert on civil liberties and criminal law and has been described by *Newsweek* as "the nation's most peripatetic civil liberties lawyer and one of its most distinguished defenders of individual rights." Dershowitz is a frequent public commentator on matters of freedom of expression and of due process, and is the author of eighteen books, including, most recently, *Why Terrorism Works: Understanding the Threat, Responding to the Challenge*, and hundreds of magazine and journal articles.

Paul McMasters – Paul McMasters is the First Amendment Ombudsman at the Freedom Forum in Arlington, Virginia. He speaks and writes frequently on all aspects of First Amendment rights, has appeared on various television programs, and has testified before numerous government commissions and congressional committees. Prior to joining the Freedom Forum, McMasters was the Associate Editorial Director of *USA Today*. He is also past National President of the Society of Professional Journalists.

Edwin Meese III – Edwin Meese III holds the Ronald Reagan Chair in Public Policy at the Heritage Foundation. He is also Chairman of Heritage's Center for Legal and Judicial Studies. Meese is a Distinguished Visiting Fellow at the Hoover Institution at Stanford University, and a Distinguished Senior Fellow at The University of London's Institute of United States Studies. He is also Chairman of the governing board at George Mason University in Virginia. Meese served as the 75th Attorney General of the United States under the Reagan Administration.

Roger Pilon – Roger Pilon is Vice President for Legal Affairs at the Cato Institute, where he holds the B. Kenneth Simon Chair in Constitutional Studies, directs Cato's Center for Constitutional Studies, and publishes the *Cato Supreme Court Review*. Prior to joining Cato, he held five senior posts in the Reagan Administration. He has taught philosophy and law, and was a National Fellow at Stanford's Hoover Institution. Pilon has published widely in moral, political, and legal theory.

Jamin Raskin – Jamin Raskin is Professor of Law at American University Washington College of Law, specializing in constitutional law and the First Amendment. He served as a member of the Clinton-Gore Justice Department Transition Team, as Assistant Attorney General in the Commonwealth of Massachusetts and as General Counsel for the National Rainbow Coalition. Raskin has also been a Teaching Fellow in the Government Department at Harvard University and has won several awards for his scholarly essays and journal articles. He is author of *We the Students* and founder of the Marshall-Brennan Fellows Program, which sends law students into public high schools to teach the Constitution.

Nadine Strossen – Nadine Strossen is President of the American Civil Liberties Union and Professor of Law at New York Law School. Strossen has published approximately 250 works in scholarly and general interest publications, and she is the author of two significant books on the importance of civil liberties to the struggle for equality. She has lectured and practiced extensively in the areas of constitutional law and civil liberties, and is a frequent commentator in the national media on various legal issues.

ABOUT FIRE

FIRE's mission is to defend, sustain, and restore individual rights at America's colleges and universities. These rights include freedom of speech, legal equality, due process, religious liberty, and sanctity of conscience—the essential qualities of civil liberty and human dignity. FIRE's core goals are to protect the unprotected against repressive behavior and partisan policies of all kinds, to educate the public about the threat to individual rights that exists on our campuses, and to lead the way in the necessary and moral effort to preserve the rights of students and faculty to speak their minds, to honor their consciences, and to be treated honestly, fairly, and equally by their institutions.

FIRE is a charitable and educational tax-exempt foundation within the meaning of Section 501 (c) (3) of the Internal Revenue Code. Contributions to FIRE are deductible to the fullest extent provided by tax laws. FIRE is funded entirely through individual donations; we receive no government funding. Please visit **www.thefire.org** for more information about FIRE.

FÎRE

David French
President

Greg Lukianoff
Director of Legal and Public Advocacy

Alan Charles Kors
Cofounder and Chairman

Harvey A. Silverglate
Cofounder and Vice Chairman

Board of Directors

William J. Hume
Joseph M. Maline
Marlene Mieske
Virginia Postrel
Ed Snider

Alan Charles Kors
Michael Meyers
Daphne Patai
Harvey A. Silverglate
James E. Wiggins

Kenny J. Williams (deceased, 2003)

KNOW YOUR RIGHTS PROGRAM:
FIRE's *GUIDES* TO STUDENT RIGHTS ON CAMPUS PROJECT

FIRE believes it imperative that our nation's future leaders be educated as members of a free society, able to debate and resolve peaceful differences without resort to repression. Toward that end, FIRE implemented its pathbreaking *Guides* to Student Rights on Campus Project.

The creation and distribution of these *Guides* is indispensable to challenging and ending the climate of censorship and enforced self-censorship on our college campuses, a climate profoundly threatening to the future of this nation's full enjoyment of and preservation of liberty. We trust that these *Guides* will enable a wholly new kind of discourse on college and university campuses.

A distinguished group of legal scholars serves as Board of Editors to this series. The board, selected from across the political and ideological spectrum, has advised FIRE on each of the *Guides*. The diversity of this board proves that liberty on campus is not a question of partisan politics, but of the rights and responsibilities of free individuals in a society governed by the rule of law.

It is our liberty, above all else, that defines us as human beings, capable of ethics and responsibility. The struggle for liberty on American campuses is one of the defining struggles of the age in which we find ourselves. A nation that does not educate in freedom will not survive in freedom and will not even know when it has lost it. Individuals too often convince themselves that they are caught up in moments of history that they cannot affect. That history, however, is made by their will and moral choices. There is a moral crisis in higher education. It will not be resolved unless we choose and act to resolve it. We invite you to join our fight.

Please visit **www.thefireguides.org** for more information on FIRE's *Guides* to Student Rights on Campus.

CONTACTING FIRE
www.thefire.org

Send inquiries, comments, and documented instances of betrayals of free speech, individual liberty, religious freedom, the rights of conscience, legal equality, due process, and academic freedom on campus to:

FIRE's website:
www.thefire.org

By email:
fire@thefire.org

By mail:
601 Walnut Street, Suite 510
Philadelphia, PA 19106

By phone/fax:
215-717-FIRE (3473) (phone)
215-717-3440 (fax)

AUTHOR

David A. French, President of the Foundation for Individual Rights in Education, is a graduate of Harvard Law School. He is also author of *A Season for Justice: Defending the Rights of the Christian Home, Church and School* (Broadman & Holman, 2002). Mr. French has extensive experience representing religious individuals and groups and served as counsel for InterVarsity Christian Fellowship's Religious Freedom Crisis Team. Mr. French has taught at Cornell Law School and was a member of the FIRE Legal Network.